The Ha[...] Journal

A daily workbook to help you use the most effective Positive Psychology techniques to radically change your life!

Journal Easy

© 2015

Happiness Journal Number:

Introduction

"Happiness is not the belief that we don't need to change; it is the realization that we can" – Shawn Achor

This journal was originally inspired by the TED talk and teachings of Shawn Achor (see link in the resources), one of the pre-eminent speakers and educators in the world of Positive Psychology.

Positive Psychology has become an increasingly important aspect of modern psychology and a way to increase success, efficiency and happiness for individuals in schools, colleges, work places and in life in general. It has also been used very successfully to help people who are struggling with depression.

Positive Psychology interventions or practices are *"treatment methods or intentional activities aimed at cultivating positive feelings, behaviors or cognitions to significantly enhance well-being and ameliorate depressive symptoms"* (Lyubomirsky)

It is important to be aware that Positive Psychology is not just a set of theories and inspiring research projects but is also a collection of very effective practices and exercises that can be used by anyone who wishes to raise their level of well-being, positive emotions and happiness. BUT for these to work, it is essential that you take action and actually commit to doing them. Without such a commitment, they are just a set of nice ideas. **This is why this journal is so important and helpful.**

Many of us search for greater happiness in life, mostly via the (conditioned) acquisition of things or the pursuit of success. But it turns out that these do not lead to lasting happiness. Ownership of more things does not correlate to increased happiness. Hoping to be happy after we have succeeded at something is a lost cause because as soon as we succeed then the goal posts are moved and we are left chasing happiness on the other side of new goals.

It turns out that the old wisdom that taught that happiness comes from within was completely right. It has also been shown that being happier leads to greater success and achievement in life, not that success and achievement will necessarily cause happiness. So now that we have the scientific data to verify and understand it, we can finally believe it and start to take the actions that support happiness to grow in our lives.

This book has been laid out in a way that makes some of the most effective fundamental daily practices of Positive Psychology really easy to do.

In the light of the research that shows that it is best not to try to do too much if you want to develop new positive habits (and this journal is all about creating new habits), the daily writings that you are encouraged to do are quite minimal in terms of quantity and time required but nevertheless they are highly effective.

If completed daily, these exercises will begin to recondition your mind's thought patterns and start to have an impact, even within a few weeks.

Wishing you a wonderful, empowering and joyful journey with your Happiness Journal.

How To Use This Journal

In the summary of his talk, Shawn suggested five basic practices to do daily, if possible, to have a powerful, positive effect on your mind that would lead to greater success, efficiency and happiness in your life. They are primarily to:

1. Write down three things that you can be grateful for in your life. These should be done first thing in the morning.
2. Write down at least one positive experience that you can appreciate that has happened to you during the day. This should be done last thing at night.

And also to:

3. Meditate.
4. Do some form of exercise.
5. Reach out to your social network and make a connection to one person who you can express appreciation to or just honor that connection in some way.

This journal is laid out in a way that allows you to do all of these things and to easily keep a record of it too.

The morning gratitudes and evening appreciation are the two most important parts of this process. It is recommended that you give priority to doing these every day. If you are also able to do any or all of the other three practices that is great but make sure that you write your gratitudes and appreciations every day as your primary commitment

The Morning Gratitudes

Writing gratitudes actually does not take very long to do at all and can often be completed within a few minutes. Plus, the more that you do it, the easier it gets because your mind becomes more used to scanning for things to be grateful for and appreciate in your daily living.

The suggestion is to **write down a minimum of 3 things that you feel grateful for in your life every morning**. They don't have to be massive things, they can be simple experiences, people or things (e.g. this can be as simple as being grateful for the comfortable bed and sheets that you have just woken up in).

As you get more used to doing this you can write more than just 3 gratitudes each day if you would like to. You can also deepen the experience if you have the time and energy by describing what the qualities of that experience, person or thing that you appreciate or enjoy are.

The best time to do these is first thing in the morning and it can be really helpful to start thinking about which gratitudes you might write down when you first awaken but before you get up.

Make it easy by keeping this journal by your bed with a pen beside it. In this way, it will make it much easier to do and to remember, as well as to form into a daily habit.

To deepen this practice further it can be really helpful to start to become consciously aware of and to appreciate these positive experiences more fully during the day, as they happen. This will help prepare you for the next daily practice...

The Evening Appreciation

Write down your appreciation for one positive experience that you have had during the day (again, you can write more if you feel so inspired). Write this at the end of the day. The best time to do this is in the evening or last thing before you go to sleep.

Meditation

Regular Meditation has been found to be incredibly effective at raising people's daily levels of positivity and happiness. It has also been found to be excellent for improving health, reducing stress, boosting creativity and increasing longevity – all of which are great extra benefits.

But don't worry if you do not know how to meditate because even very simple meditations like just watching your breath for 10 minutes can have a powerful effect.

There are also some phenomenal sound technologies that have been developed that will automatically drop your brain into a meditative state without you even having to do anything. The easiest one can be done by just listening to a 12 minute track of music or sounds. There is some great information about these at: www.modernmeditator.com

Within this journal you just need to tick next to where "Meditation" is written on the page if you did do any. If you want, you might like to keep a record of how many minutes of meditation you did or how many times you took a brief meditation break through your day. It's up to you.

Exercise

There is a lot of research into the effectiveness of exercise as a powerful anti-depressant (in fact it has been shown to be as effective as anti-depressant drugs in the short term and more effective than them in the long term!) Exercise will release endorphins (the feel good hormones) into your system which helps create natural positivity and reduce anxiety. Plus, as we all know, exercise is really good for our body's health on many levels.

It is recommended that you choose a form of exercise that you will enjoy (forcing yourself to do exercise that you don't enjoy is likely to be ineffective and counterproductive) and just commit to a minimal amount at first. Do something at least 3 x per week. This can be increased if and when you feel inspired to do more. Deciding the night before what exercise you will do, as well as when and where, will make it easier to just do it.

It can also help if you choose a form of exercise that is fun or that you can do with others socially.

In the journal you just need to place a tick next to where it says "Exercise". If you wish you could write down what you did, how much or how long too.

Social Connection

The final happiness practice that you can start to include is to consciously choose to connect with people in your social circles or family. In many ways, social support is your single biggest asset. The "Very Happy People" research project (2002) sought to discover what was common between very happy people across the world and the only thing that they all had in common was strong social relationships.

When making connections consciously as part of your journey to greater happiness with this workbook, they should be made with the intention of expressing appreciation of some positive aspect of your friends or the relationship that you have with that person or also perhaps as an exercise that allows you to reconnect with friends that you have been out of touch with.

This does not have to be any major form of communication. It may be as simple as a text or a brief email. It could be a phone call or a skype session. Sometimes it may be that you actually take the time out to go out and meet up with that person for a chat or a lovely/fun shared experience.

In the journal next to "Social Connection" you can write the name of the person that you reached out to and perhaps note the quality that you acknowledged in them or what you did together, if this is relevant.

Date

I am grateful for...

My favorite Positive experience(s) for today was (were)...

Meditation: Exercise:

Social Connection:

Date

I am grateful for...

My favorite Positive experience(s) for today was (were)...

Meditation: Exercise:

Social Connection:

<u>Date</u>

I am grateful for...

My favorite Positive experience(s) for today was (were)...

<u>Meditation:</u>   <u>Exercise:</u>

<u>Social Connection:</u>

<u>Date</u>

I am grateful for...

My favorite Positive experience(s) for today was (were)...

<u>Meditation:</u>   <u>Exercise:</u>

<u>Social Connection:</u>

<u>Date</u>

I am grateful for...

My favorite Positive experience(s) for today was (were)...

<u>Meditation:</u>   <u>Exercise:</u>

<u>Social Connection:</u>

<u>Date</u>

I am grateful for...

My favorite Positive experience(s) for today was (were)...

<u>Meditation:</u>   <u>Exercise:</u>

<u>Social Connection:</u>

Date

I am grateful for...

My favorite Positive experience(s) for today was (were)...

Meditation: Exercise:

Social Connection:

_____

Date

I am grateful for...

My favorite Positive experience(s) for today was (were)...

Meditation: Exercise:

Social Connection:

Date

I am grateful for...

My favorite Positive experience(s) for today was (were)...

Meditation: Exercise:

Social Connection:

Date

I am grateful for...

My favorite Positive experience(s) for today was (were)...

Meditation: Exercise:

Social Connection:

<u>Date</u>

I am grateful for...

My favorite Positive experience(s) for today was (were)...

<u>Meditation:</u>   <u>Exercise:</u>

<u>Social Connection:</u>

_____

<u>Date</u>

I am grateful for...

My favorite Positive experience(s) for today was (were)...

<u>Meditation:</u>   <u>Exercise:</u>

<u>Social Connection:</u>

Date

I am grateful for...

My favorite Positive experience(s) for today was (were)...

Meditation: Exercise:

Social Connection:

Date

I am grateful for...

My favorite Positive experience(s) for today was (were)...

Meditation: Exercise:

Social Connection:

<u>Date</u>

I am grateful for...

My favorite Positive experience(s) for today was (were)...

<u>Meditation:</u>   <u>Exercise:</u>

<u>Social Connection:</u>
_____

<u>Date</u>

I am grateful for...

My favorite Positive experience(s) for today was (were)...

<u>Meditation:</u>   <u>Exercise:</u>

<u>Social Connection:</u>

Date

I am grateful for...

My favorite Positive experience(s) for today was (were)...

Meditation: Exercise:

Social Connection:

Date

I am grateful for...

My favorite Positive experience(s) for today was (were)...

Meditation: Exercise:

Social Connection:

<u>Date</u>

I am grateful for...

My favorite Positive experience(s) for today was (were)...

<u>Meditation:</u>   <u>Exercise:</u>

<u>Social Connection:</u>

_____

<u>Date</u>

I am grateful for...

My favorite Positive experience(s) for today was (were)...

<u>Meditation:</u>   <u>Exercise:</u>

<u>Social Connection:</u>

Date

I am grateful for...

My favorite Positive experience(s) for today was (were)...

Meditation: Exercise:

Social Connection:

Date

I am grateful for...

My favorite Positive experience(s) for today was (were)...

Meditation: Exercise:

Social Connection:

Date

I am grateful for...

My favorite Positive experience(s) for today was (were)...

Meditation: Exercise:

Social Connection:

_____

Date

I am grateful for...

My favorite Positive experience(s) for today was (were)...

Meditation: Exercise:

Social Connection:

Date

I am grateful for...

My favorite Positive experience(s) for today was (were)...

Meditation: Exercise:

Social Connection:

Date

I am grateful for...

My favorite Positive experience(s) for today was (were)...

Meditation: Exercise:

Social Connection:

Date

I am grateful for...

My favorite Positive experience(s) for today was (were)...

Meditation: Exercise:

Social Connection:

_____

Date

I am grateful for...

My favorite Positive experience(s) for today was (were)...

Meditation: Exercise:

Social Connection:

<u>Date</u>

I am grateful for...

My favorite Positive experience(s) for today was (were)...

<u>Meditation:</u>   <u>Exercise:</u>

<u>Social Connection:</u>

<u>Date</u>

I am grateful for...

My favorite Positive experience(s) for today was (were)...

<u>Meditation:</u>   <u>Exercise:</u>

<u>Social Connection:</u>

<u>Date</u>

I am grateful for...

My favorite Positive experience(s) for today was (were)...

<u>Meditation:</u>   <u>Exercise:</u>

<u>Social Connection:</u>

_____

<u>Date</u>

I am grateful for...

My favorite Positive experience(s) for today was (were)...

<u>Meditation:</u>   <u>Exercise:</u>

<u>Social Connection:</u>

Date

I am grateful for...

My favorite Positive experience(s) for today was (were)...

Meditation: Exercise:

Social Connection:

Date

I am grateful for...

My favorite Positive experience(s) for today was (were)...

Meditation: Exercise:

Social Connection:

Date

I am grateful for...

My favorite Positive experience(s) for today was (were)...

Meditation: Exercise:

Social Connection:

_____

Date

I am grateful for...

My favorite Positive experience(s) for today was (were)...

Meditation: Exercise:

Social Connection:

Date

I am grateful for...

My favorite Positive experience(s) for today was (were)...

Meditation: Exercise:

Social Connection:

Date

I am grateful for...

My favorite Positive experience(s) for today was (were)...

Meditation: Exercise:

Social Connection:

<u>Date</u>

I am grateful for...

My favorite Positive experience(s) for today was (were)...

<u>Meditation:</u>   <u>Exercise:</u>

<u>Social Connection:</u>

_____

<u>Date</u>

I am grateful for...

My favorite Positive experience(s) for today was (were)...

<u>Meditation:</u>   <u>Exercise:</u>

<u>Social Connection:</u>

<u>Date</u>

I am grateful for...

My favorite Positive experience(s) for today was (were)...

<u>Meditation:</u>   <u>Exercise:</u>

<u>Social Connection:</u>

<u>Date</u>

I am grateful for...

My favorite Positive experience(s) for today was (were)...

<u>Meditation:</u>   <u>Exercise:</u>

<u>Social Connection:</u>

Date

I am grateful for...

My favorite Positive experience(s) for today was (were)...

Meditation: Exercise:

Social Connection:

_____

Date

I am grateful for...

My favorite Positive experience(s) for today was (were)...

Meditation: Exercise:

Social Connection:

<u>Date</u>

I am grateful for...

My favorite Positive experience(s) for today was (were)...

<u>Meditation:</u>   <u>Exercise:</u>

<u>Social Connection:</u>

<u>Date</u>

I am grateful for...

My favorite Positive experience(s) for today was (were)...

<u>Meditation:</u>   <u>Exercise:</u>

<u>Social Connection:</u>

Date

I am grateful for...

My favorite Positive experience(s) for today was (were)...

Meditation: Exercise:

Social Connection:

_____

Date

I am grateful for...

My favorite Positive experience(s) for today was (were)...

Meditation: Exercise:

Social Connection:

Date

I am grateful for...

My favorite Positive experience(s) for today was (were)...

Meditation: Exercise:

Social Connection:

Date

I am grateful for...

My favorite Positive experience(s) for today was (were)...

Meditation: Exercise:

Social Connection:

<u>Date</u>

I am grateful for...

My favorite Positive experience(s) for today was (were)...

<u>Meditation:</u>   <u>Exercise:</u>

<u>Social Connection:</u>

_____

<u>Date</u>

I am grateful for...

My favorite Positive experience(s) for today was (were)...

<u>Meditation:</u>   <u>Exercise:</u>

<u>Social Connection:</u>

Date

I am grateful for...

My favorite Positive experience(s) for today was (were)...

Meditation: Exercise:

Social Connection:

Date

I am grateful for...

My favorite Positive experience(s) for today was (were)...

Meditation: Exercise:

Social Connection:

Date

I am grateful for...

My favorite Positive experience(s) for today was (were)...

Meditation: Exercise:

Social Connection:

_____

Date

I am grateful for...

My favorite Positive experience(s) for today was (were)...

Meditation: Exercise:

Social Connection:

Date

I am grateful for...

My favorite Positive experience(s) for today was (were)...

Meditation: Exercise:

Social Connection:

Date

I am grateful for...

My favorite Positive experience(s) for today was (were)...

Meditation: Exercise:

Social Connection:

<u>Date</u>

I am grateful for...

My favorite Positive experience(s) for today was (were)...

<u>Meditation:</u>   <u>Exercise:</u>

<u>Social Connection:</u>

<u>Date</u>

I am grateful for...

My favorite Positive experience(s) for today was (were)...

<u>Meditation:</u>   <u>Exercise:</u>

<u>Social Connection:</u>

Date

I am grateful for...

My favorite Positive experience(s) for today was (were)...

Meditation: Exercise:

Social Connection:

Date

I am grateful for...

My favorite Positive experience(s) for today was (were)...

Meditation: Exercise:

Social Connection:

Date

I am grateful for...

My favorite Positive experience(s) for today was (were)...

Meditation: Exercise:

Social Connection:

_____

Date

I am grateful for...

My favorite Positive experience(s) for today was (were)...

Meditation: Exercise:

Social Connection:

Date

I am grateful for...

My favorite Positive experience(s) for today was (were)...

Meditation: Exercise:

Social Connection:

Date

I am grateful for...

My favorite Positive experience(s) for today was (were)...

Meditation: Exercise:

Social Connection:

Date

I am grateful for...

My favorite Positive experience(s) for today was (were)...

Meditation: Exercise:

Social Connection:

_____

Date

I am grateful for...

My favorite Positive experience(s) for today was (were)...

Meditation: Exercise:

Social Connection:

Date

I am grateful for...

My favorite Positive experience(s) for today was (were)...

Meditation: Exercise:

Social Connection:

Date

I am grateful for...

My favorite Positive experience(s) for today was (were)...

Meditation: Exercise:

Social Connection:

Date

I am grateful for...

My favorite Positive experience(s) for today was (were)...

Meditation: Exercise:

Social Connection:

_____

Date

I am grateful for...

My favorite Positive experience(s) for today was (were)...

Meditation: Exercise:

Social Connection:

<u>Date</u>

I am grateful for...

My favorite Positive experience(s) for today was (were)...

<u>Meditation:</u>   <u>Exercise:</u>

<u>Social Connection:</u>

<u>Date</u>

I am grateful for...

My favorite Positive experience(s) for today was (were)...

<u>Meditation:</u>   <u>Exercise:</u>

<u>Social Connection:</u>

Date

I am grateful for…

My favorite Positive experience(s) for today was (were)…

Meditation: Exercise:

Social Connection:

_____

Date

I am grateful for…

My favorite Positive experience(s) for today was (were)…

Meditation: Exercise:

Social Connection:

Date

I am grateful for...

My favorite Positive experience(s) for today was (were)...

Meditation: Exercise:

Social Connection:

Date

I am grateful for...

My favorite Positive experience(s) for today was (were)...

Meditation: Exercise:

Social Connection:

Date

I am grateful for...

My favorite Positive experience(s) for today was (were)...

Meditation: Exercise:

Social Connection:

_____

Date

I am grateful for...

My favorite Positive experience(s) for today was (were)...

Meditation: Exercise:

Social Connection:

<u>Date</u>

I am grateful for...

My favorite Positive experience(s) for today was (were)...

<u>Meditation:</u>   <u>Exercise:</u>

<u>Social Connection:</u>

<u>Date</u>

I am grateful for...

My favorite Positive experience(s) for today was (were)...

<u>Meditation:</u>   <u>Exercise:</u>

<u>Social Connection:</u>

Date

I am grateful for...

My favorite Positive experience(s) for today was (were)...

Meditation: Exercise:

Social Connection:

_____

Date

I am grateful for...

My favorite Positive experience(s) for today was (were)...

Meditation: Exercise:

Social Connection:

Date

I am grateful for...

My favorite Positive experience(s) for today was (were)...

Meditation: Exercise:

Social Connection:

Date

I am grateful for...

My favorite Positive experience(s) for today was (were)...

Meditation: Exercise:

Social Connection:

Date

I am grateful for...

My favorite Positive experience(s) for today was (were)...

Meditation: Exercise:

Social Connection:

_____

Date

I am grateful for...

My favorite Positive experience(s) for today was (were)...

Meditation: Exercise:

Social Connection:

Date

I am grateful for...

My favorite Positive experience(s) for today was (were)...

Meditation: Exercise:

Social Connection:

Date

I am grateful for...

My favorite Positive experience(s) for today was (were)...

Meditation: Exercise:

Social Connection:

Date

I am grateful for...

My favorite Positive experience(s) for today was (were)...

Meditation: Exercise:

Social Connection:

_____

Date

I am grateful for...

My favorite Positive experience(s) for today was (were)...

Meditation: Exercise:

Social Connection:

Date

I am grateful for...

My favorite Positive experience(s) for today was (were)...

Meditation: Exercise:

Social Connection:

Date

I am grateful for...

My favorite Positive experience(s) for today was (were)...

Meditation: Exercise:

Social Connection:

<u>Date</u>

I am grateful for...

My favorite Positive experience(s) for today was (were)...

<u>Meditation:</u>   <u>Exercise:</u>

<u>Social Connection:</u>

_____

<u>Date</u>

I am grateful for...

My favorite Positive experience(s) for today was (were)...

<u>Meditation:</u>   <u>Exercise:</u>

<u>Social Connection:</u>

<u>Date</u>

I am grateful for...

My favorite Positive experience(s) for today was (were)...

<u>Meditation:</u>   <u>Exercise:</u>

<u>Social Connection:</u>

<u>Date</u>

I am grateful for...

My favorite Positive experience(s) for today was (were)...

<u>Meditation:</u>   <u>Exercise:</u>

<u>Social Connection:</u>

Date

I am grateful for...

My favorite Positive experience(s) for today was (were)...

Meditation: Exercise:

Social Connection:

_____

Date

I am grateful for...

My favorite Positive experience(s) for today was (were)...

Meditation: Exercise:

Social Connection:

<u>Date</u>

I am grateful for...

My favorite Positive experience(s) for today was (were)...

<u>Meditation:</u>   <u>Exercise:</u>

<u>Social Connection:</u>

<u>Date</u>

I am grateful for...

My favorite Positive experience(s) for today was (were)...

<u>Meditation:</u>   <u>Exercise:</u>

<u>Social Connection:</u>

<u>Date</u>

I am grateful for...

My favorite Positive experience(s) for today was (were)...

<u>Meditation:</u>   <u>Exercise:</u>

<u>Social Connection:</u>

<u>Date</u>

I am grateful for...

My favorite Positive experience(s) for today was (were)...

<u>Meditation:</u>   <u>Exercise:</u>

<u>Social Connection:</u>

Date

I am grateful for...

My favorite Positive experience(s) for today was (were)...

Meditation: Exercise:

Social Connection:

Date

I am grateful for...

My favorite Positive experience(s) for today was (were)...

Meditation: Exercise:

Social Connection:

Date

I am grateful for...

My favorite Positive experience(s) for today was (were)...

Meditation: Exercise:

Social Connection:

_____

Date

I am grateful for...

My favorite Positive experience(s) for today was (were)...

Meditation: Exercise:

Social Connection:

Date

I am grateful for...

My favorite Positive experience(s) for today was (were)...

Meditation: Exercise:

Social Connection:

Date

I am grateful for...

My favorite Positive experience(s) for today was (were)...

Meditation: Exercise:

Social Connection:

Date

I am grateful for...

My favorite Positive experience(s) for today was (were)...

Meditation: Exercise:

Social Connection:

_____

Date

I am grateful for...

My favorite Positive experience(s) for today was (were)...

Meditation: Exercise:

Social Connection:

Date

I am grateful for...

My favorite Positive experience(s) for today was (were)...

Meditation: Exercise:

Social Connection:

Date

I am grateful for...

My favorite Positive experience(s) for today was (were)...

Meditation: Exercise:

Social Connection:

Date

I am grateful for...

My favorite Positive experience(s) for today was (were)...

Meditation: Exercise:

Social Connection:

_____

Date

I am grateful for...

My favorite Positive experience(s) for today was (were)...

Meditation: Exercise:

Social Connection:

Date

I am grateful for...

My favorite Positive experience(s) for today was (were)...

Meditation: Exercise:

Social Connection:

Date

I am grateful for...

My favorite Positive experience(s) for today was (were)...

Meditation: Exercise:

Social Connection:

Date

I am grateful for...

My favorite Positive experience(s) for today was (were)...

Meditation: Exercise:

Social Connection:

_____

Date

I am grateful for...

My favorite Positive experience(s) for today was (were)...

Meditation: Exercise:

Social Connection:

Date

I am grateful for...

My favorite Positive experience(s) for today was (were)...

Meditation: Exercise:

Social Connection:

_____

Date

I am grateful for...

My favorite Positive experience(s) for today was (were)...

Meditation: Exercise:

Social Connection:

<u>Date</u>

I am grateful for...

My favorite Positive experience(s) for today was (were)...

<u>Meditation:</u>   <u>Exercise:</u>

<u>Social Connection:</u>

_____

<u>Date</u>

I am grateful for...

My favorite Positive experience(s) for today was (were)...

<u>Meditation:</u>   <u>Exercise:</u>

<u>Social Connection:</u>

Date

I am grateful for...

My favorite Positive experience(s) for today was (were)...

Meditation: Exercise:

Social Connection:

Date

I am grateful for...

My favorite Positive experience(s) for today was (were)...

Meditation: Exercise:

Social Connection:

Date

I am grateful for...

My favorite Positive experience(s) for today was (were)...

Meditation: Exercise:

Social Connection:

_____

Date

I am grateful for...

My favorite Positive experience(s) for today was (were)...

Meditation: Exercise:

Social Connection:

Date

I am grateful for...

My favorite Positive experience(s) for today was (were)...

Meditation: Exercise:

Social Connection:

_____

Date

I am grateful for...

My favorite Positive experience(s) for today was (were)...

Meditation: Exercise:

Social Connection:

Date

I am grateful for...

My favorite Positive experience(s) for today was (were)...

Meditation: Exercise:

Social Connection:

_____

Date

I am grateful for...

My favorite Positive experience(s) for today was (were)...

Meditation: Exercise:

Social Connection:

Date

I am grateful for...

My favorite Positive experience(s) for today was (were)...

Meditation: Exercise:

Social Connection:

Date

I am grateful for...

My favorite Positive experience(s) for today was (were)...

Meditation: Exercise:

Social Connection:

Date

I am grateful for...

My favorite Positive experience(s) for today was (were)...

Meditation: Exercise:

Social Connection:

_____

Date

I am grateful for...

My favorite Positive experience(s) for today was (were)...

Meditation: Exercise:

Social Connection:

Date

I am grateful for...

My favorite Positive experience(s) for today was (were)...

Meditation: Exercise:

Social Connection:

Date

I am grateful for...

My favorite Positive experience(s) for today was (were)...

Meditation: Exercise:

Social Connection:

Date

I am grateful for...

My favorite Positive experience(s) for today was (were)...

Meditation: Exercise:

Social Connection:

_____

Date

I am grateful for...

My favorite Positive experience(s) for today was (were)...

Meditation: Exercise:

Social Connection:

Date

I am grateful for...

My favorite Positive experience(s) for today was (were)...

Meditation: Exercise:

Social Connection:

Date

I am grateful for...

My favorite Positive experience(s) for today was (were)...

Meditation: Exercise:

Social Connection:

Date

I am grateful for...

My favorite Positive experience(s) for today was (were)...

Meditation: Exercise:

Social Connection:

_____

Date

I am grateful for...

My favorite Positive experience(s) for today was (were)...

Meditation: Exercise:

Social Connection:

Date

I am grateful for...

My favorite Positive experience(s) for today was (were)...

Meditation: Exercise:

Social Connection:

Date

I am grateful for...

My favorite Positive experience(s) for today was (were)...

Meditation: Exercise:

Social Connection:

Date

I am grateful for...

My favorite Positive experience(s) for today was (were)...

Meditation: Exercise:

Social Connection:

Date

I am grateful for...

My favorite Positive experience(s) for today was (were)...

Meditation: Exercise:

Social Connection:

<u>Date</u>

I am grateful for...

My favorite Positive experience(s) for today was (were)...

<u>Meditation:</u>   <u>Exercise:</u>

<u>Social Connection:</u>

_____

<u>Date</u>

I am grateful for...

My favorite Positive experience(s) for today was (were)...

<u>Meditation:</u>   <u>Exercise:</u>

<u>Social Connection:</u>

Date

I am grateful for...

My favorite Positive experience(s) for today was (were)...

Meditation: Exercise:

Social Connection:

_____

Date

I am grateful for...

My favorite Positive experience(s) for today was (were)...

Meditation: Exercise:

Social Connection:

Date

I am grateful for...

My favorite Positive experience(s) for today was (were)...

Meditation: Exercise:

Social Connection:

Date

I am grateful for...

My favorite Positive experience(s) for today was (were)...

Meditation: Exercise:

Social Connection:

Date

I am grateful for...

My favorite Positive experience(s) for today was (were)...

Meditation: Exercise:

Social Connection:

_____

Date

I am grateful for...

My favorite Positive experience(s) for today was (were)...

Meditation: Exercise:

Social Connection:

Date

I am grateful for...

My favorite Positive experience(s) for today was (were)...

Meditation: Exercise:

Social Connection:

_____

Date

I am grateful for...

My favorite Positive experience(s) for today was (were)...

Meditation: Exercise:

Social Connection:

<u>Date</u>

I am grateful for...

My favorite Positive experience(s) for today was (were)...

<u>Meditation:</u>   <u>Exercise:</u>

<u>Social Connection:</u>

_____

<u>Date</u>

I am grateful for...

My favorite Positive experience(s) for today was (were)...

<u>Meditation:</u>   <u>Exercise:</u>

<u>Social Connection:</u>

Date

I am grateful for...

My favorite Positive experience(s) for today was (were)...

Meditation: Exercise:

Social Connection:

Date

I am grateful for...

My favorite Positive experience(s) for today was (were)...

Meditation: Exercise:

Social Connection:

Date

I am grateful for…

My favorite Positive experience(s) for today was (were)…

Meditation: Exercise:

Social Connection:

_____

Date

I am grateful for…

My favorite Positive experience(s) for today was (were)…

Meditation: Exercise:

Social Connection:

<u>Date</u>

I am grateful for...

My favorite Positive experience(s) for today was (were)...

<u>Meditation:</u> <u>Exercise:</u>

<u>Social Connection:</u>

<u>Date</u>

I am grateful for...

My favorite Positive experience(s) for today was (were)...

<u>Meditation:</u> <u>Exercise:</u>

<u>Social Connection:</u>

Date

I am grateful for...

My favorite Positive experience(s) for today was (were)...

Meditation: Exercise:

Social Connection:

_____

Date

I am grateful for...

My favorite Positive experience(s) for today was (were)...

Meditation: Exercise:

Social Connection:

Date

I am grateful for...

My favorite Positive experience(s) for today was (were)...

Meditation: Exercise:

Social Connection:

Date

I am grateful for...

My favorite Positive experience(s) for today was (were)...

Meditation: Exercise:

Social Connection:

Date

I am grateful for...

My favorite Positive experience(s) for today was (were)...

Meditation: Exercise:

Social Connection:

_____

Date

I am grateful for...

My favorite Positive experience(s) for today was (were)...

Meditation: Exercise:

Social Connection:

Date

I am grateful for...

My favorite Positive experience(s) for today was (were)...

Meditation: Exercise:

Social Connection:

Date

I am grateful for...

My favorite Positive experience(s) for today was (were)...

Meditation: Exercise:

Social Connection:

Date

I am grateful for...

My favorite Positive experience(s) for today was (were)...

Meditation: Exercise:

Social Connection:

_____

Date

I am grateful for...

My favorite Positive experience(s) for today was (were)...

Meditation: Exercise:

Social Connection:

Date

I am grateful for...

My favorite Positive experience(s) for today was (were)...

Meditation: Exercise:

Social Connection:

Date

I am grateful for...

My favorite Positive experience(s) for today was (were)...

Meditation: Exercise:

Social Connection:

Date

I am grateful for...

My favorite Positive experience(s) for today was (were)...

Meditation: Exercise:

Social Connection:

_____

Date

I am grateful for...

My favorite Positive experience(s) for today was (were)...

Meditation: Exercise:

Social Connection:

<u>Date</u>

I am grateful for...

My favorite Positive experience(s) for today was (were)...

<u>Meditation:</u>   <u>Exercise:</u>

<u>Social Connection:</u>

<u>Date</u>

I am grateful for...

My favorite Positive experience(s) for today was (were)...

<u>Meditation:</u>   <u>Exercise:</u>

<u>Social Connection:</u>

Date

I am grateful for…

My favorite Positive experience(s) for today was (were)…

Meditation: Exercise:

Social Connection:

Date

I am grateful for…

My favorite Positive experience(s) for today was (were)…

Meditation: Exercise:

Social Connection:

Date

I am grateful for...

My favorite Positive experience(s) for today was (were)...

Meditation: Exercise:

Social Connection:

Date

I am grateful for...

My favorite Positive experience(s) for today was (were)...

Meditation: Exercise:

Social Connection:

<u>Date</u>

I am grateful for...

My favorite Positive experience(s) for today was (were)...

<u>Meditation:</u>   <u>Exercise:</u>

<u>Social Connection:</u>

_____

<u>Date</u>

I am grateful for...

My favorite Positive experience(s) for today was (were)...

<u>Meditation:</u>   <u>Exercise:</u>

<u>Social Connection:</u>

Date

I am grateful for...

My favorite Positive experience(s) for today was (were)...

Meditation: Exercise:

Social Connection:

Date

I am grateful for...

My favorite Positive experience(s) for today was (were)...

Meditation: Exercise:

Social Connection:

<u>Date</u>

I am grateful for...

My favorite Positive experience(s) for today was (were)...

<u>Meditation:</u>   <u>Exercise:</u>

<u>Social Connection:</u>

_____

<u>Date</u>

I am grateful for...

My favorite Positive experience(s) for today was (were)...

<u>Meditation:</u>   <u>Exercise:</u>

<u>Social Connection:</u>

Date

I am grateful for...

My favorite Positive experience(s) for today was (were)...

Meditation: Exercise:

Social Connection:

Date

I am grateful for...

My favorite Positive experience(s) for today was (were)...

Meditation: Exercise:

Social Connection:

Date

I am grateful for...

My favorite Positive experience(s) for today was (were)...

Meditation: Exercise:

Social Connection:

_____

Date

I am grateful for...

My favorite Positive experience(s) for today was (were)...

Meditation: Exercise:

Social Connection:

Date

I am grateful for...

My favorite Positive experience(s) for today was (were)...

Meditation: Exercise:

Social Connection:

Date

I am grateful for...

My favorite Positive experience(s) for today was (were)...

Meditation: Exercise:

Social Connection:

Date

I am grateful for...

My favorite Positive experience(s) for today was (were)...

Meditation: Exercise:

Social Connection:

Date

I am grateful for...

My favorite Positive experience(s) for today was (were)...

Meditation: Exercise:

Social Connection:

<u>Date</u>

I am grateful for...

My favorite Positive experience(s) for today was (were)...

<u>Meditation:</u>   <u>Exercise:</u>

<u>Social Connection:</u>

<u>Date</u>

I am grateful for...

My favorite Positive experience(s) for today was (were)...

<u>Meditation:</u>   <u>Exercise:</u>

<u>Social Connection:</u>

<u>Date</u>

I am grateful for...

My favorite Positive experience(s) for today was (were)...

<u>Meditation:</u>   <u>Exercise:</u>

<u>Social Connection:</u>

_____

<u>Date</u>

I am grateful for...

My favorite Positive experience(s) for today was (were)...

<u>Meditation:</u>   <u>Exercise:</u>

<u>Social Connection:</u>

Date

I am grateful for...

My favorite Positive experience(s) for today was (were)...

Meditation: Exercise:

Social Connection:

_____

Date

I am grateful for...

My favorite Positive experience(s) for today was (were)...

Meditation: Exercise:

Social Connection:

<u>Date</u>

I am grateful for…

My favorite Positive experience(s) for today was (were)…

<u>Meditation:</u>   <u>Exercise:</u>

<u>Social Connection:</u>

_____

<u>Date</u>

I am grateful for…

My favorite Positive experience(s) for today was (were)…

<u>Meditation:</u>   <u>Exercise:</u>

<u>Social Connection:</u>

<u>Date</u>

I am grateful for...

My favorite Positive experience(s) for today was (were)...

<u>Meditation:</u>   <u>Exercise:</u>

<u>Social Connection:</u>

<u>Date</u>

I am grateful for...

My favorite Positive experience(s) for today was (were)...

<u>Meditation:</u>   <u>Exercise:</u>

<u>Social Connection:</u>

Date

I am grateful for...

My favorite Positive experience(s) for today was (were)...

Meditation: Exercise:

Social Connection:

_____

Date

I am grateful for...

My favorite Positive experience(s) for today was (were)...

Meditation: Exercise:

Social Connection:

Date

I am grateful for...

My favorite Positive experience(s) for today was (were)...

Meditation: Exercise:

Social Connection:

Date

I am grateful for...

My favorite Positive experience(s) for today was (were)...

Meditation: Exercise:

Social Connection:

<u>Date</u>

I am grateful for...

My favorite Positive experience(s) for today was (were)...

<u>Meditation:</u>   <u>Exercise:</u>

<u>Social Connection:</u>

_____

<u>Date</u>

I am grateful for...

My favorite Positive experience(s) for today was (were)...

<u>Meditation:</u>   <u>Exercise:</u>

<u>Social Connection:</u>

Date

I am grateful for...

My favorite Positive experience(s) for today was (were)...

Meditation: Exercise:

Social Connection:

Date

I am grateful for...

My favorite Positive experience(s) for today was (were)...

Meditation: Exercise:

Social Connection:

<u>Date</u>

I am grateful for...

My favorite Positive experience(s) for today was (were)...

<u>Meditation:</u>   <u>Exercise:</u>

<u>Social Connection:</u>

_____

<u>Date</u>

I am grateful for...

My favorite Positive experience(s) for today was (were)...

<u>Meditation:</u>   <u>Exercise:</u>

<u>Social Connection:</u>

Date

I am grateful for...

My favorite Positive experience(s) for today was (were)...

Meditation: Exercise:

Social Connection:

Date

I am grateful for...

My favorite Positive experience(s) for today was (were)...

Meditation: Exercise:

Social Connection:

Date

I am grateful for...

My favorite Positive experience(s) for today was (were)...

Meditation: Exercise:

Social Connection:

_____

Date

I am grateful for...

My favorite Positive experience(s) for today was (were)...

Meditation: Exercise:

Social Connection:

Date

I am grateful for...

My favorite Positive experience(s) for today was (were)...

Meditation: Exercise:

Social Connection:

Date

I am grateful for...

My favorite Positive experience(s) for today was (were)...

Meditation: Exercise:

Social Connection:

Date

I am grateful for...

My favorite Positive experience(s) for today was (were)...

Meditation: Exercise:

Social Connection:

_____

Date

I am grateful for...

My favorite Positive experience(s) for today was (were)...

Meditation: Exercise:

Social Connection:

Date

I am grateful for...

My favorite Positive experience(s) for today was (were)...

Meditation;   Exercise:

Social Connection:

Date

I am grateful for...

My favorite Positive experience(s) for today was (were)...

Meditation: Exercise:

Social Connection:

Date

I am grateful for...

My favorite Positive experience(s) for today was (were)...

Meditation: Exercise:

Social Connection:

_____

Date

I am grateful for...

My favorite Positive experience(s) for today was (were)...

Meditation: Exercise:

Social Connection:

Date

I am grateful for...

My favorite Positive experience(s) for today was (were)...

Meditation: Exercise:

Social Connection:

Date

I am grateful for...

My favorite Positive experience(s) for today was (were)...

Meditation: Exercise:

Social Connection:

Date

I am grateful for…

My favorite Positive experience(s) for today was (were)…

Meditation: Exercise:

Social Connection:

_____

Date

I am grateful for…

My favorite Positive experience(s) for today was (were)…

Meditation: Exercise:

Social Connection:

Date

I am grateful for...

My favorite Positive experience(s) for today was (were)...

Meditation: Exercise:

Social Connection:

Date

I am grateful for...

My favorite Positive experience(s) for today was (were)...

Meditation: Exercise:

Social Connection:

<u>Date</u>

I am grateful for…

My favorite Positive experience(s) for today was (were)…

<u>Meditation:</u>   <u>Exercise:</u>

<u>Social Connection:</u>

_____

<u>Date</u>

I am grateful for…

My favorite Positive experience(s) for today was (were)…

<u>Meditation:</u>   <u>Exercise:</u>

<u>Social Connection:</u>

<u>Date</u>

I am grateful for...

My favorite Positive experience(s) for today was (were)...

<u>Meditation:</u>   <u>Exercise:</u>

<u>Social Connection:</u>

<u>Date</u>

I am grateful for...

My favorite Positive experience(s) for today was (were)...

<u>Meditation:</u>   <u>Exercise:</u>

<u>Social Connection:</u>

<u>Date</u>

I am grateful for...

My favorite Positive experience(s) for today was (were)...

<u>Meditation:</u>   <u>Exercise:</u>

<u>Social Connection:</u>

_____

<u>Date</u>

I am grateful for...

My favorite Positive experience(s) for today was (were)...

<u>Meditation:</u>   <u>Exercise:</u>

<u>Social Connection:</u>

Date

I am grateful for...

My favorite Positive experience(s) for today was (were)...

Meditation: Exercise:

Social Connection:

Date

I am grateful for...

My favorite Positive experience(s) for today was (were)...

Meditation: Exercise:

Social Connection:

Date

I am grateful for...

My favorite Positive experience(s) for today was (were)...

Meditation: Exercise:

Social Connection:

_____

Date

I am grateful for...

My favorite Positive experience(s) for today was (were)...

Meditation: Exercise:

Social Connection:

Date

I am grateful for...

My favorite Positive experience(s) for today was (were)...

Meditation: Exercise:

Social Connection:

Date

I am grateful for...

My favorite Positive experience(s) for today was (were)...

Meditation: Exercise:

Social Connection:

Date

I am grateful for...

My favorite Positive experience(s) for today was (were)...

Meditation: Exercise:

Social Connection:

_____

Date

I am grateful for...

My favorite Positive experience(s) for today was (were)...

Meditation: Exercise:

Social Connection:

<u>Date</u>

I am grateful for...

My favorite Positive experience(s) for today was (were)...

<u>Meditation:</u>   <u>Exercise:</u>

<u>Social Connection:</u>

<u>Date</u>

I am grateful for...

My favorite Positive experience(s) for today was (were)...

<u>Meditation:</u>   <u>Exercise:</u>

<u>Social Connection:</u>

<u>Date</u>

I am grateful for...

My favorite Positive experience(s) for today was (were)...

<u>Meditation:</u>   <u>Exercise:</u>

<u>Social Connection:</u>

_____

<u>Date</u>

I am grateful for...

My favorite Positive experience(s) for today was (were)...

<u>Meditation:</u>   <u>Exercise:</u>

<u>Social Connection:</u>

Date

I am grateful for...

My favorite Positive experience(s) for today was (were)...

Meditation: Exercise:

Social Connection:

Date

I am grateful for...

My favorite Positive experience(s) for today was (were)...

Meditation: Exercise:

Social Connection:

<u>Date</u>

I am grateful for...

My favorite Positive experience(s) for today was (were)...

<u>Meditation:</u>   <u>Exercise:</u>

<u>Social Connection:</u>

_____

<u>Date</u>

I am grateful for...

My favorite Positive experience(s) for today was (were)...

<u>Meditation:</u>   <u>Exercise:</u>

<u>Social Connection:</u>

Date

I am grateful for...

My favorite Positive experience(s) for today was (were)...

Meditation: Exercise:

Social Connection:

Date

I am grateful for...

My favorite Positive experience(s) for today was (were)...

Meditation: Exercise:

Social Connection:

Date

I am grateful for...

My favorite Positive experience(s) for today was (were)...

Meditation: Exercise:

Social Connection:

Date

I am grateful for...

My favorite Positive experience(s) for today was (were)...

Meditation: Exercise:

Social Connection:

Date

I am grateful for...

My favorite Positive experience(s) for today was (were)...

Meditation: Exercise:

Social Connection:

Date

I am grateful for...

My favorite Positive experience(s) for today was (were)...

Meditation: Exercise:

Social Connection:

Date

I am grateful for...

My favorite Positive experience(s) for today was (were)...

Meditation: Exercise:

Social Connection:

_____

Date

I am grateful for...

My favorite Positive experience(s) for today was (were)...

Meditation: Exercise:

Social Connection:

Date

I am grateful for...

My favorite Positive experience(s) for today was (were)...

Meditation: Exercise:

Social Connection:

Date

I am grateful for...

My favorite Positive experience(s) for today was (were)...

Meditation: Exercise:

Social Connection:

<u>Date</u>

I am grateful for...

My favorite Positive experience(s) for today was (were)...

<u>Meditation:</u>   <u>Exercise:</u>

<u>Social Connection:</u>

_____

<u>Date</u>

I am grateful for...

My favorite Positive experience(s) for today was (were)...

<u>Meditation:</u>   <u>Exercise:</u>

<u>Social Connection:</u>

Date

I am grateful for...

My favorite Positive experience(s) for today was (were)...

Meditation: Exercise:

Social Connection:

Date

I am grateful for...

My favorite Positive experience(s) for today was (were)...

Meditation: Exercise:

Social Connection:

Date

I am grateful for...

My favorite Positive experience(s) for today was (were)...

Meditation: Exercise:

Social Connection:

_____

Date

I am grateful for...

My favorite Positive experience(s) for today was (were)...

Meditation: Exercise:

Social Connection:

Date

I am grateful for...

My favorite Positive experience(s) for today was (were)...

Meditation: Exercise:

Social Connection:

Date

I am grateful for...

My favorite Positive experience(s) for today was (were)...

Meditation: Exercise:

Social Connection:

Date

I am grateful for...

My favorite Positive experience(s) for today was (were)...

Meditation: Exercise:

Social Connection:

_____

Date

I am grateful for...

My favorite Positive experience(s) for today was (were)...

Meditation: Exercise:

Social Connection:

Resources

Watch Shawn Achor's original inspiring TED talk at:
https://www.youtube.com/watch?v=fLJsdqxnZb0

Books by Shawn Achor:

- The Happiness Advantage

- Before Happiness

Meditation Made Easy

For some really helpful information, as well as music and tools to make the practice of meditation much easier, I would encourage you to go and check out www.modernmeditator.com

(Especially look out for the discount offers they have on the 12 minute meditation recordings).